Merci

What is washi tape?

Washi tape is a low-tack, decorative paper
tape that can (and should) be used on everything!
The word *washi* refers to the Japanese paper from which
the tape is made. Known simply as masking tape in Japan,
it can be layered for various effects, as most of it is slightly
transparent, and can be used to create large designs for
home décor or placed on a quick piece of correspondence for
an instant pop of color. While washi tape originated in Japan,
it is now made throughout the world.

What is in this kit?

- 2 rolls of coordinating, patterned washi tape

- 12 white postcards

- 2 fine-line permanent markers in black and pink

How to use washi tape

TEARING OR CUTTING

Washi tape can be torn or cut. The deckled, irregular torn edge can add to the handmade look of a project. Cut the edges of the tape with scissors for a clean edge, use pinking shears for a zigzag edge, or tear the tape with a tape dispenser, for a tiny serrated edge.

To create shapes like small triangles, squares, or arrow-tipped ends use scissors to freehand cut the tape.

When making detailed shapes or trimming tape in place (for example, on a surface), use a dull craft knife to score the tape, then tear it away for a clean line.

CREATING PATTERNED SHEETS

To create patterned sheets, layer tape onto waxed paper, overlapping strips of tape slightly. Create a solid sheet of all one kind of tape or vary colors, widths, and patterns to create your own design.

Freehand cut shapes with
scissors, cut detailed shapes with a craft knife and
cutting mat, or punch shapes with craft punches.

CREATING PLAIDS

Using washi tape to create plaids is a great way to start playing with color without pressure. Let go and experiment with the transparency of the tape and learn how solids create unique colors and patterns as they overlap. There are no rules for making fun and funky plaids. Create cards, postcards, or little framable works of art.

WRITING ON WASHI TAPE

The fine-line permanent markers in this kit will write on both the postcard surface as well as on the washi tape. Note that washi tape has a lightly waxy surface that will only take permanent inks. Allow the ink to dry a few moments before touching or rubbing over the tape on your project. Dark inks show up best on the tapes, but experiment with various ink colors for different effects. Use the pink pen for writing and drawing on the postcard itself.

More fun with washi tape!

Here are some more fun ideas of ways to use washi tape.

PATTERNED POSTCARD

To make additional postcards, cut them from cardstock. Use washi tape to create your own design. Vary thick and thin tapes and alternate between patterns and solids to create a dynamic composition.

Add characters or little critters by using tape with animals or stylized creatures printed on it. Add a stamp and pop it into the mail!

BIRTHDAY CARD

Whip up a cute little cupcake for a birthday card. Using 1½" (3.5 cm) -wide solid tape, cut out a frosting shape and layer a patterned cupcake wrapper made from patchwork tape on top. Complete with a washi tape candle. Make an enclosure card with the same methods in miniature.

 Use rubber stamps to create your own special greeting.

CELEBRATION CARD

Buntings are the epitome of party décor. Make a card that says "celebration" instantly. Draw three softly swooping lines across your card. Cut triangles from various solid and patterned washi tapes to create bunting flags of all styles. Place the flags along your drawn lines to create three-tiered buntings. Because the tape is low tack, you can move the flags around until you have the perfect arrangement.

QUICK AND EASY THANK YOU

Keep a couple of tiny thank-you notes handy in your bag; you never know when someone will surprise you and you'll want to say thank you for being awesome. A little square of paper goes from scrappy to special with a border of washi tape. Tuck a thank-you note into a pocket, leave it on a seat, or add it to a bouquet of wildflowers.

CAMPFIRE INVITE

An impromptu summer sleepover is the perfect excuse to eat s'mores! Create a camping-themed invite to inspire a night of stargazing and roasting marshmallows over the fire.

Let kids decorate their own invites or make them together for a family craft night.

MEMORIES AND MEMENTOS—ART JOURNALING

Keeping an art journal or daily record of your life can feel like a lot of pressure on some days. Using washi tape for both decoration and utility is a surefire way to attack a couple of pages before dinner. Add little bits of paper ephemera such as bus tickets, movie stubs, photos, and notes with washi tape. Use tape to frame out quotes or thoughts, edge pages, or hold down photos.

QUARRY

The author can be found on Instagram (#101washitape)
and on Twitter (@ccerruti)

Design: Mattie S. Wells
Photography: Matthieu Brajot

ISBN: 978-1-63159-002-3

Printed in 2014
2 4 6 8 10 9 7 5 3 1
www.quartous.com